A TO Z LIVING LIFE, GOD'S WAY

D. Lafe

WestBow Press books may be ordered through booksellers or by contacting:

WestBow Press
A Division of Thomas Nelson & Zondervan
1663 Liberty Drive
Bloomington, IN 47403
www.westbowpress.com
844-714-3454

ISBN: 978-1-6642-7155-5 (sc)
ISBN: 978-1-6642-7156-2 (e)

Library of Congress Control Number: 2022912381

Print information available on the last page.

WestBow Press rev. date: 11/26/2022

WESTBOW
PRESS®
A DIVISION OF THOMAS NELSON
& ZONDERVAN

I dedicate this book to J, my miracle, my blessing, my teacher, and my son.

Your name means thankful. Thank God in everything, J! ☺

Dear readers,

I admire your desire to use the word of God to determine your path in life. Some of you are parents or caregivers who bought this book to help your children live according to God's precepts.

The message of the book is consistently woven throughout each piece of advice. God made you for his glory and wants to save and fulfill you, so live life according to his plan, not yours.

The main content of the book is divided into three columns. The first column gives practical advice using each letter of the alphabet. In essence, column 1 says to do this or that. WHY? Because God says so, as seen in column 3.

Column 3 is the most important column in the book. It gives the biblical reason or framework for the advice. We should do this or that because God tells us to do so.

Column 2 makes the book interactive. Below each image, there is space for you to solidify your understanding of the advice and the scripture and ensure deeper involvement and learning. You can put your own artwork/drawings or glue pictures and objects that reflect the scriptures and the advice in order to make it relevant to your everyday life. You can also jot down ideas or reflections related to your life in this space as well.

Whether reading this book with your child or reading it alone, the goal is to appreciate the advice and scriptures as concrete concepts relevant to our everyday lives and have fun doing so.

It is also to encourage discussion. One of the best things we can do for our kids is to help them navigate life by directly and experientially showing them how God's words can guide them. Let us be available to answer their questions and help them find the same through prayer and the word of God. If you are reading this alone, seek a trusted adult or mentor to help you engage more deeply with God's word.

This book can be used by very young readers or by older children. The bolded section at the beginning of each advice is better suited for young readers to fit their attention span and level of understanding. The more detailed expansion that follows each advice is geared towards older children.

It is not intended to be read only once. It is designed to be a book that is revisited. As children grow older, they can continue to use it to gain even deeper insights and memorize more verses. They can also change the images or memorabilia used in previous readings to fit their current situation.

Activity pages are also included at the back of the book to give you an opportunity to further engage with the content. The goal is for the children to continue to interact with the word of God.

May Almighty God continue to bless you as you live life, in His way. Ready, Set, Go! :)

D. Lafe

Prayer for the dear readers

Heavenly Father, my wonderful and awesome creator, I praise you today. I glorify your name and acknowledge you as sovereign, as King. I exalt you. You are the Great I am, and I thank you for giving us salvation and the power to enjoy an abundant life. You deserve all praise and adoration.

I pray that you will touch the readers' hearts profoundly so that they will grow more in love with you with each passing day. That love, when encouraged in the heart of a child, can sustain him/her for a lifetime and into eternity. Proverbs 22:6 (NIV) implores caregivers and parents to 'Start children off on the way they should go, and even when they are old, they will not turn from it.'

Whatever their trajectory through life, 'the way they should go' is rooted in your word. 2 Timothy3:16-17 (ESV) tells us that all scripture is breathed out by God and profitable for teaching, for reproof, for correction, and for training in righteousness, that the man of God may be competent, equipped for every good work.'

Dear Lord, may the children reading this book be fully equipped to live their lives to bring you glory. May they be trained in righteous living. I claim all of that for them in your son's precious name.

May you strengthen and comfort the caregivers, parents, and the children as they run this race of life. May your words be indelibly stamped on their hearts so that they will use them as their daily guidepost to live a life that is pleasing to you. 2 Timothy 3:15 (NKJV) declares that when you learn the word of God from childhood that it is 'able to make you wise for salvation through faith which is in Christ Jesus.' I pray that the children will become wise as they learn and apply your word at every stage of their lives.

I thank you for answering my prayer, in Jesus' name. Amen.

Always thank God for the good things that happen to you. He loves you very much and wants the best for you.

Always, always thank God in everything. No matter what the situation, he has a plan for you.

God has done so much for you, from creating you, to offering you his awesome gift of salvation, to helping you daily with all aspects of your life. All the things you take for granted, like food, clothes, shelter, the love of family and friends, health, and air are attributable to God's love, grace, and provisions. If you were to stop and itemize every positive thing he has done, you would have a very long list. Please stop right now and thank him. Repeat this process every day. You will realize that your list will start getting longer. God deserves our gratitude.

There is also an added blessing that accompanies a grateful heart. When you are thankful, you complain less and your outlook on life becomes more positive. This positivity spills over into all areas of your life and makes you more likable and encouraging to others.

Give thanks in all circumstances; for this is God's will for you in Christ Jesus. 1 Thessalonians 5:18 NIV

Every good and perfect gift is from above, coming down from the Father of the heavenly lights, who does not change like shifting shadows. James 1:17 NIV

Give thanks to the Lord for he is good; his love endures forever. Psalm 107:1 NIV

What happens, though, when bad things happen, which they naturally do? The advice is the same. Thank God in every situation. You are thanking him for helping you through the bad, for his comfort and strength, and the good that he will engineer out of it to bless you. We live in a fallen world so evil is present and sometimes we are affected.

God has a plan for that too. He is never taken off guard. You can thank him for his help even before things improve because, without a doubt, he is working behind the scenes to help you.

In good times and in bad, always, always thank him.

Be nice to others by helping them.

God is love, and his love is tangible. How can we tell? He gave his only son, his best gift, to us simply because he loves us so much and did not want to see us suffer eternity without him. As believers, we, too, must show tangible love to others. It's not enough to say that we love people. We must show them through our actions. How do we do that? We do that by being nice.

How can we be nice throughout our day? We can do so by

- smiling
- listening
- donating
- helping with tasks
- encouraging
- spending time with others
- volunteering
- buying gifts

The list is endless.

People need to see God's love through us. It is one of the most important ways we can show others that we care about them. Your response to others must be kind and welcoming. Anything other than this may make people believe God is unfeeling and uncaring. Show them just how kind and approachable Almighty God is. **Be nice to people.**

Do not neglect to do good and to share what you have, for such sacrifices are pleasing to God. Hebrews 13:16 ESV

Whoever is generous to the poor lends to the Lord, and he will repay him for his deed. Proverbs 19:17 ESV

A new commandment I give to you, that you love one another: just as I have loved you, you also are to love one another. John 13:34 -ESV

Cheer your friends on when they are trying something new or challenging.

When others think that people are on their team or want them to succeed, they feel bold to face challenges. When you do so, your friends will feel more confident as they embark on new projects, try out a novel activity, or take a test. We all face challenges in life and will continue to do so,

Cheer them up when they are sad or lonely.

The Holy Spirit is our Comforter. We can look to Him in our darkest moments. We are never alone because God is always with us. He wants us to comfort others with the same comfort he gives us.

Look around you. You will find many opportunities to comfort and encourage others. Since everyone faces challenges, we should prepare ourselves to share God's comfort so they can know that they, too, are not alone.

So, be there for others as they weather the storms of life and let them know that God is always there to help them through the difficulties and that you, as his humble servant, will also encourage and cheer them on.

Cheer on and cheer up other people.

Therefore encourage one another and build one another up, just as you are doing. (1 Thessalonians 5:11- ESV)

Who comforts us in all our affliction, so that we may be able to comfort those who are in any affliction, with the comfort with which we ourselves are comforted by God. 2 Corinthians 1:4-ESV

Do your best to use the gifts and talents God gave you to help yourself and others.

God created us to serve him. He loves us and wants to give us eternal life in heaven. He has gifted us with various talents, so we can serve him by serving the people he loves.

Our God is a giver and wants us to follow his lead. He wants us to use our natural talents to point others to him and help with their everyday needs. Using our talents and gifts only to satisfy ourselves is inconsistent with the way God wants us to live. God GAVE his very best, his son, to the world so that he could save us and fill us with his love and power to be a blessing to others.

Like a good father, he wants us to imitate him as our model. Use the gifts God generously gave you to serve him with all your heart. You may think that you are not gifted, but you certainly are! The Almighty creator gave you abilities that seem to come naturally to you. In addition to asking God for his guidance, you can also ask your close friends, acquaintances, and family members about what they think are your natural abilities. That will help you to discover your areas of strength. Ask God to increase your motivation to improve these skills to serve him wholeheartedly and effectively.

Do your best with your gifts!

Whatever you do, work heartily, as for the Lord and not for men. Colossians 3:23-ESV

For even the Son of Man came not to be served but to serve, and to give his life as a ransom for many. Mark 10:45 -ESV

For you were called to freedom, brothers. Only do not use your freedom as an opportunity for the flesh, but through love serve one another. Galatians 5:13-ESV

Encourage others when they feel • disappointed • frustrated • rejected • sad • scared		Therefore encourage one another and build one another up, just as you are doing. 1 Thessalonians 5:11 -ESV
When God made Adam, he concluded that Adam needed companionship. The God of the universe acknowledged our need for a deep bond with another person. He strategized to ensure Adam could meet that need with Eve's help. The same is true for you and me. It is even more critical when faced with strong emotions that sadden and confuse us. We do so much better with the support of others. How can you do this? Be a good listener. Sometimes the best encouragement you can provide is your quiet presence. By listening to the person as he/she shares, without judgment, his/her burden can become lighter to bear. Let them know you are praying for them. Prayer can be uplifting when people realize you are going to God on their behalf. Sometimes, when they hear you pray aloud for them, they feel more encouraged. God cares about our mental state. He cares when we cry and when we feel defeated. The Bible is full of verses that encourage us through our difficult moments. He wants us, through how we live our lives, to show the world that there is hope in him and that they matter to him. Encourage others!		9 Two are better than one, because they have a good return for their labor: 10 If either of them falls down, one can help the other up. But pity anyone who falls and has no one to help them up. Ecclesiastes 4:9-10-NIV
		Not neglecting to meet together, as is the habit of some, but encouraging one another, and all the more as you see the Day drawing near. Hebrews 10:25-ESV

Face challenges with bravery. When you pray, God will always give you the strength to do your best. Step out in faith.

Is life hard? Sometimes it is. Sometimes challenges are not dire. They are just new experiences that present great opportunities for you to learn. These times may make you feel both excited and scared at the same time. Know that you can trust God to help you amid uncertainty. He does not want fear to cripple you from achieving your best. Ask God for his wisdom and walk in confidence that the God of the universe has your back. Whatever the outcome, he will use it for good, for his glory.

However, sometimes the challenges seem downright terrible, such as the case of a loved one hurting or dying. Trust in God with all your heart that he will help you. He sees you, and he certainly understands how you are feeling. He watched his son die on the cross so you could have eternity with him. Tragic occurrences happen because we live in a fallen world where the devil is devising plans to destroy us. However, what the devil means for evil, God has strategized to create good. Remember, trust him.

You may feel defeated and all alone when you experience physical or emotional hurt. Know this. When Jesus was on the cross and felt abandoned by his Father, his Father already had the plan of salvation worked out. He has not left you and never will. Your pain will not go unnoticed. He has a plan.

Face all challenges confidently because God is with you.

Have I not commanded you? Be strong and courageous. Do not be afraid; do not be discouraged, for the LORD your God will be with you wherever you go." Joshua 1:9 NIV

I can do all things through him who strengthens me. Philippians 4:13-ESV

Fear not, for I am with you; be not dismayed, for I am your God; I will strengthen you, I will help you, I will uphold you with my righteous right hand. Isaiah 41:10-ESV

Now faith is the confidence in what we hope for and assurance about what we do not see. Hebrews 11:1-NIV

Go to someone who loves you when you need help and advice.

When you need advice, pray about it first. Ask God for his wisdom. He promises to help. Ask him to direct you to others who will assist you in making godly decisions. Many voices may tell you what decisions to make. However, ignore the advice that focuses on your abilities or what the masses believe. How do you know who to trust?

Look at the people around you, for those who

- have consistently helped you to make good decisions
- are helping you to make decisions that glorify God

Please do not decide to do something because everyone else is doing it. Reflect on what will please God. Search his word for clarity and ask trusted friends and adults for their godly insight.

God did not create you to live your life isolated and in mental anguish. He created you to be a light, an example to the world. To do so, you will need godly counsel from those who have endured and overcome. Listen and take heed. Look upward to God for his divine intervention and look outward to others who can remind you and challenge you to follow the Lord in all that you do.

Go and find godly advice.

If any of you lacks wisdom, you should ask God, who gives generously to all without finding fault, and it will be given to you. James 1:5 NIV

Whoever walks with the wise becomes wise, but the companion of fools will suffer harm. Proverbs 13:20-ESV

Where there is no guidance, a people falls, but in an abundance of counselors there is safety. Proverbs 11:14-ESV

Help others to understand that God loves them and wants to help them.

God does not want anyone to perish and suffer eternal separation from him. He created the salvation strategy in which Jesus would take our punishment and free us from condemnation, guilt, shame, and eternal punishment, the inevitable consequences of our sins. Having done that and given us his nature, he wants the world to know about this incredible gift so others can receive it and live a transformed life with the ultimate gift of everlasting life.

We are privileged to be the bearers of good news. You can use your words to tell others about this and point them to the bible. Let your actions reflect his transformative power. When others see the change in your life, they will be curious to know why. Prepare to tell them.

The world needs to know that God loves them. Some may feel scared that they have done too many bad things and that God cannot accept them. Please tell them the truth that Jesus died specifically for them and that his death was an act of love to save them from their sins and to give them hope now and for eternity.

Have the confidence to share this good news with others. Where they spend eternity may depend on your willingness to talk to them about their true worth in Christ and their eternal destiny.

Help others by sharing God's plan of salvation with them.

Go therefore and make disciples of all the nations, baptizing them in the name of the Father and of the Son and of the Holy Spirit, teaching them to observe all things that I have commanded you; and lo, I am with you always, even to the end of the age." Matthew 28:19-20 NKJV

If we confess our sins, he is faithful and just to forgive us our sins and to cleanse us from all unrighteousness. 1 John 1:9-ESV

For God so loved the world, that he gave his only Son, that whoever believes in him should not perish but have eternal life. John 3:16-ESV

Invite others to play with you and be part of your group. Please include them in your activities and do good things together.

Therefore welcome one another as Christ has welcomed you, for the glory of God. Romans 15:7-ESV

Oh, how God loves us! He allowed his precious son to die for us. He tells us to love each other. If we prayerfully, do it his way, we will feel honored to be kind to his people and to include them in our activities.

This is my commandment, that you love one another as I have loved you. John 15:12-ESV

It is natural for a person to feel sad and rejected when he/she is excluded from a group. God has called you to counteract such a situation. He expects you to ensure that your actions do not belittle the extraordinary masterpiece that each person is, according to his design. What then can you do?

Do not be deceived: "Bad company ruins good morals." 1 Corinthians 15:33 ESV

Include, include, include. Since your mission is to serve God and his people, your activities will tend to be praiseworthy. If you involve others in such activities, you are not only making them feel loved and accepted, but you will be getting help to create more good work for God.

When you see a peer who regularly sits alone, invite him/her to spend time with you and your friends. You and your friends may be the only ones who 'noticed' him/her in quite a while.

Look out for the lonely. God's people are hurting alone and need Jesus to rescue them. You can be that bridge between their despair and the hope that Jesus provides. Invite them to your church or to spend time with your group so they can experience God's unconditional love and acceptance.

Invite and include others.

Just be you. You are one of a kind. God loves and values you very much. Do not try to be just like everyone else or anyone else. Be who God has called you to be. Jesus died to save you.

Of all the people in the world, you are unique. That is simply amazing. No one is exactly like you. You are a wonder that only Almighty God could have envisioned. The intricate physical and mental details of your framework are simply unmatched. You are a rare specimen of infinite importance to God. If all this is true, and it is, there is no reason to try to be just like someone else because the real you is more special than a counterfeit of another person.

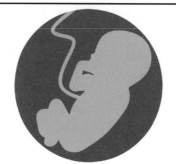

For you formed my inward parts; you knitted me together in my mother's womb. I praise you, for I am fearfully and wonderfully made. Wonderful are your works; my soul knows it very well. My frame was not hidden from you, when I was being made in secret, intricately woven in the depths of the earth. Your eyes saw my unformed substance; in your book were written, every one of them, the days that were formed for me, when as yet there was none of them. Psalm 139:13-16 ESV

Why, even the hairs of your head are all numbered. Fear not; you are of more value than many sparrows. Luke 12:7-ESV

For God so loved the world, that he gave his only Son, that whoever believes in him should not perish but have eternal life. John 3:16 -ESV

If that is extraordinary, also think of your importance to God. That is mindboggling. He loves you so much. Yes, you! He suffered so much via his son's sacrifice to ensure that you can live a fulfilled and ever-lastingly glorious life. He did it for you. If the God of the universe considers you that important, you too should agree with him in his assessment of who you are.

When self-esteem issues arise, remind yourself of this fact. When rejection threatens to derail your confidence, remind yourself of who your creator is, what he did during your design process, what he does now to assist you in your day-to-day life, and what he has orchestrated for you for the afterlife.

Meditate on your uniqueness, and remember that you are important enough for Christ to have died for you. Take it all in and bless God for his wisdom and creativity. You are one of a kind. So, **just be you**.

Kind words are the best words to use even when you disagree with someone.

K.I.N.D.

Know that when you interact with someone, you are dealing with God's masterpiece.
Imagine God as a silent observer of the conversation.
Nip harsh words from your vocabulary.
Develop the discipline of using inspiring words that Jesus would use.

Our words are powerful. They can do great harm, or they can be very uplifting to the hearer. They can encourage or cripple for decades. With that much power, you will need to control and manage what you say to benefit the hearer. Speak the truth but do so in a way to build others up, not to tear them down and make them feel insignificant. The goal should never be to win the argument to appear more intelligent but to show God's love through your words.

Do not let any unwholesome talk come out of your mouths, but only what is helpful for building others up according to their needs, that it may benefit those who listen. Ephesians 4:29 NIV

But now you must put them all away: anger, wrath, malice, slander, and obscene talk from your mouth. Colossians 3:8- ESV

Whoever belittles his neighbor lacks sense. Proverbs 11:12- ESV

Gracious words are like a honeycomb, sweetness to the soul and health to the body. Proverbs 16:24 -ESV

A soft answer turns away wrath, but a harsh word stirs up anger. Proverbs 15:1-ESV

It is relatively easy to criticize, judge, and gossip. Our sinful nature allows this effortlessly. With Christ in our lives, we are new creations that can control our tongue. Use that power to edify others with your words. God knows the positive impact of positive comments. It is little wonder that he repeatedly urges us to watch what we say and to season our speech with kindness.

Since we are so uniquely different, we will inevitably have different opinions. It is okay to have a different viewpoint without resorting to insults. Practice doing this. The more you practice, the more mature you will become. As you disagree and sometimes vehemently, you should express yourself respectfully and kindly. Leave the person's dignity intact after the discussion.

Remember, be K.I.N.D **with your words.**

Love God with <u>all your heart.</u> Love others as you love yourself.

Whatever you do, wherever you go, the essential thing you should do is to love the Lord with every fiber of your being. Nothing or no one else should take first place in your life. He should be the center around which everything else revolves. As your creator and your redeemer, he should be your King.

Think of the person that you love the most. You want to spend time with the person. You also want to make the person proud. Your love for God must be much greater than what you would give to anyone here on Earth. For all he has done, he deserves this honor. Without him, you would not have been here. He can and will save you if you ask. You cannot live a fulfilled life without him. Once he has his rightful place as your number one priority, you can live a balanced life knowing that you will not lose your way by idolizing anyone or anything.

Love the Lord your God with all your heart and with all your soul and with all your mind and with all your strength. Mark 12:30 -NIV

For I command you today to love the Lord your God, to walk in obedience to him, and to keep his commands, decrees and laws; then you will live and increase, and the Lord your God will bless you in the land you are entering to possess. Deuteronomy 30:16-NIV

This is my commandment, that you love one another as I have loved you. John 15:12-ESV

Praise the Lord, my soul; all my inmost being, praise his holy name. Psalm 103:1-NIV

Once God has the central control in your life, he wants you to love others. He loves us so much that he wants others to care about us too. Our heavenly father has promised to bless us as we bless others. He understands how good you will feel when you love and help others.

On every level, this is a win-win for you. You get to be a blessing and be blessed as you help others. Did you know that when you focus on attending to other people's needs, your troubles do not seem so insurmountable? Of course, you should not neglect your needs to become a people pleaser. You are not showing them attention to get anything from them. You are doing it because God asks you to do it, and you want to please him because you love him with all your heart. **Love God and love people, in that order.**

Make God the center of your life. Let him guide you in everything you do.

With God as your guide, you can chart your life well. He should be the captain of your ship, the chef in your kitchen, and the driver of your car. You get the picture. Let God direct your actions. Study his words so that he can change your motivations. Your goal must be to do his will. Only then will you lead a fulfilled life.

We are all imperfect beings. We make many mistakes; some are harmless, and others have devastating and long-lasting consequences for us and others. Is it then safe to trust our judgment? No, trust God. He is infallible. He has the wisdom you want and the love you desire. He has it all. Rest in his word.

It will be tempting to follow the world's advice as seen through movies, magazines, music, friends, and others. However, if those do not lead you to follow Christ, do not let them influence you. No matter how loud it seems that others are yelling to get you to do something against God's principles, stand firm and trust God as the director of your life.

Make God your driving force.

But seek first the kingdom of God and his righteousness, and all these things will be added to you. Matthew 6:33 -ESV

Trust in the Lord with all your heart, and do not lean on your own understanding. In all your ways acknowledge him, and he will make straight your paths. Proverbs 3:5-6 -ESV

Commit your way to the Lord; trust in him, and he will act. Psalm 37:5-ESV

Never do what others do when you know God does not want you to do it. With God's help, you can stand up for what is right.

Peer influence can sometimes be good. When friends or acquaintances challenge you to do something positive for yourself and others, you are in good company. However, sometimes their influence has the opposite effect. Navigating the difference can be tricky. You may fear losing their friendship or inclusion in their group. However, their acceptance must be secondary to what God tells us to do. You should not follow friends into eternal separation from God. Pray to God to send godly friendships and individuals into your life to keep you accountable to him.

If someone is not following Christ, do not follow him/her. God will give you the strength to resist temptation and stand up for what is right. Pray and trust him to do it. You may be ridiculed, insulted, or bullied for your beliefs and godly stance. Do not give in. You have the army of God behind you. Do not believe that going along with what you know is wrong will make things easier for you. It will make it more difficult because you would have given up your will to people who do not have your best interest at heart. The consequences of your actions can sometimes take years to overcome. Pray to God every day to give you the courage for that day to triumph over sinful pressure and to help you find godly, trusted adults who can build up your courage.

Never disobey God to befriend others!

Therefore, if anyone is in Christ, he is a new creation. The old has passed away; behold, the new has come. 2 Corinthians 5:17 ESV

Don't copy the behavior and customs of this world, but let God transform you into a new person by changing the way you think. Then you will learn to know God's will for you, which is good and pleasing and perfect. Romans 12:2-NLT

Be imitators of me, as I am of Christ. Now I commend you because you remember me in everything and maintain the traditions even as I delivered them to you. 1 Corinthians 11:1-2 ESV

Organize your life.

Life is hectic. There are many things that you must get done. Your attention is being pulled in many different directions, and you may get overwhelmed. Do not despair. With God as the center, you can lead a balanced life in which you focus on the most important areas of your life. God made this universe in perfect order. The majesty of his creation is breathtaking. So many things are timed just right and are in sync with so many other things that enable us to live comfortably on earth.

If he could do that, he can certainly help you organize your hectic life. You must make him your number one priority and then pray for discernment, wisdom, and understanding. Like everything else in this universe, he made you and has a purpose for your life. Go to him to determine your every and next step.

As you focus on doing his will, you will realize that your life is not as hurried. You can find peace knowing that your next big project or your mundane tasks are all revolving in an orderly fashion around his will for your life.

When you are tempted to overcommit, make sure you have discussed your engagements with the creator of the universe. Remember, he has a plan. Your job is to follow it. By doing this, you will find peace as you become equipped to organize your life in a way that pleases the Lord.

○ Later
○ Tomorrow
○ Today
● NOW

For God is not a God of disorder but of peace, as in all the meetings of God's holy people. 1 Cor. 14:33-NLT

But be sure that everything is done properly and in order. 1 Cor. 14:40 NLT

Suppose one of you wants to build a tower. Won't you first sit down and estimate the cost to see if you have enough money to complete it? Luke 14:28-NIV

But all things should be done decently and in order. 1 Corinthians 14:40-ESV

Pray.

Develop a friendship with God by talking to him about everything. He is the best parent, friend, counselor, guide, redeemer, and protector. He is our everything. He has all this power, yet he wants to have a deep relationship with you. It does not get any better than this. There are many areas of life in which we can't readily get an appointment with people in leadership. For some, we will never get the opportunity to speak to them in our lifetime.

However, we need no such appointment with Almighty God, the God of the universe. You will not need another person to arrange a meeting. Jesus' death and resurrection ensure that you always have a welcoming seat at his table. You will always have access. Jesus' sacrifice shows a level of acceptance that is not even fathomable. The Lord actively seeks the friendship of his servants.

Compare this with the scenario painted above. How often do we see the leadership of a country or organization set aside power and prestige to pursue the regular constituent or worker actively and relentlessly? Not often. Right?

Our heavenly father does. He has made himself available to us every single second of every day. Tap into this fantastic resource. Enter his presence and bask in the glory of perfect love, guidance, and wisdom.

Pray without ceasing. 1 Thessalonians 5:17-ESV

Is anyone among you in trouble? Let them pray. Is anyone happy? Let them sing songs of praise. James 5:13-NIV

Do not be anxious about anything, but in everything by prayer and supplication with thanksgiving let your requests be made known to God. Philippians 4:6-ESV

Be a walking praying machine. Have an ongoing dialogue with God throughout your day. You do not have to wait for a perfect opportunity or circumstance to talk to your King. Wherever you are, you can whisper a prayer, silent or otherwise, as the situation warrants. He wants you to speak with him. Yes, you! He sees you, loves you, and wants to help you. Crack a smile, knowing that your heavenly father delights in your talks. Remember, he sought out Adam and Eve to spend time with them. He is seeking you. Talk to him. Listen to him.

Pray!

Quiet times with God will help you make good decisions and choices.

We make decisions based on our thoughts. When we think positively, we tend to develop an optimistic outlook. An optimistic outlook influences the actions we take and the activities we promote.

Many messages bombard us throughout the day, especially now that social media is integral to our lives. All these messages vie for our attention. These messages, sometimes covert and other times overt, are directly opposed to biblical principles. You do not have to be confused or discouraged. Meditate on God's words because this will push out the noise from the world and allow you to focus on the hope that God gives. Focusing on God's words will give you a hopeful outlook and allow you to spread this to others.

Finally, brothers, whatever is true, whatever is honorable, whatever is just, whatever is pure, whatever is lovely, whatever is commendable, if there is any excellence, if there is anything worthy of praise, think about these things. Philippians 4:8-ESV

I will meditate on your precepts and fix my eyes on your ways. Psalm 119:15-ESV

I have fought the good fight, I have finished the race, I have kept the faith. 2 Timothy 4:7-ESV

Whoever you spend the most time with, your habits will become similar to theirs. Some young people spend a lot of time listening to music and can then repeat verbatim the words of many songs sung by their preferred artiste. Others spend much time listening to different social media influencers and begin to articulate their views as their own. Still, others hang around friends and begin to adopt the same lifestyle practices. Spend time with God, and you will start to reflect his image. Jesus spent much quiet time with God and was thus able to articulate his views and fulfill his purpose.

Do the same. Put down the phone or gadget. Set aside regular time where you study the word, reflect, pray, worship, listen to God and bask in the love of your heavenly father.

Get quiet with God!

Respect others even if you disagree with them.
God made them, so he values them too.

God made us in his image. His son died so we could have everlasting life in heaven. He desires an intimate relationship with us. Although he is our master, he still treasures us. Even though we disobey him, he continues to pursue us. That shows that he values us.

As believers, we should value others as well. We do not have to agree with them or their lifestyle, but we must appreciate them as worthy of respect.

Since your goal is to please God, you should not easily be offended by what others say. If you allow yourself to be sidetracked away from your focus on God, the devil can use their words or disrespect to cause you to become resentful and angry. Once you get into this bitter stage, you can easily disrespect them.

Be respectful!

A hot-tempered person starts fights; a cool-tempered person stops them. Proverbs 15:18-NLT

By insolence comes nothing but strife, but with those who take advice is wisdom. Proverbs 13:10-ESV

Honor your father and your mother, as the Lord your God commanded you, that your days may be long, and that it may go well with you in the land that the Lord your God is giving you. Deuteronomy 5:16-ESV

Sing songs of praise to God. They will please Him and make you and others feel good.

God has been so good to you. Let him know how grateful you are as often as you can. One way to do that is to sing songs that exalt his name. Don't worry about not having a beautiful voice. He looks at your heart and will appreciate your offering of praise.

Your singing can be a personal offering of praise, or it can be public. If God blessed you with the gift of singing, do not keep this to yourself. Sing songs that will bless God and others. Many people feel close to God during worship. Using your gift, you can help others focus on God, his salvation, deliverance, and hope.

For music lovers, music impacts them on a profound level. They use it to deepen their relationship with God by singing alone or with others. As you proclaim God's goodness in song, you can dispel doubts you have, experience clarity or healing, and express your joy or frustration. God welcomes all of it. He relishes your undivided attention as you lose yourself in praise and petition to him through song.

Many non-believers spend a lot of time investing in purchasing, listening to, and attending concerts by their favorite artists. It is even more pressing for us to go above and beyond to use music to glorify God's name.

Sing to and about the Lord!

Make a joyful noise to the Lord, all the earth! Serve the Lord with gladness! Come into his presence with singing! Psalm 100:1-2 -ESV

But I will sing of your strength; I will sing aloud of your steadfast love in the morning. For you have been to me a fortress and a refuge in the day of my distress. Psalm 59:16 -ESV

I will praise the name of God with a song; I will magnify him with thanksgiving. Psalm 69:30-ESV

Take time to rest and reenergize.

When facing hardships, rest in God's promises that he will deliver you. He will be there fighting your battles. By trusting him, you will be at peace. You can get flustered, apprehensive, deflated, and depressed if you don't. You may also work so hard to overcome obstacles on your own that you become overly stressed and physically and emotionally exhausted.

When you give your burdens and trials over to him for him to fix them, you can live with the peace and assurance that he will guide you to make the best decisions to further his will. With him in control, you can rest. You can wait patiently for his deliverance and live with hope.

Once you have given over your worries to him and have prioritized him in your life, you do not have to overburden yourself. You can relax with renewed hope. In that way, you can renew your spirits and be prepared to fulfill God's destiny for your life.

It is a marvel to be at peace amidst the storms of life when you put your trust in the Lord.

Take time to relax, knowing that God is your defender!

Come to me, all of you who are weary and carry heavy burdens, and I will give you rest. Matt. 11:28-ESV

But they who wait on the LORD shall renew their strength; They shall mount up with wings like eagles, they shall run and not be weary, they shall walk and not faint. Isaiah 40:31-ESV

Wait on the LORD; Be of good courage, and He shall strengthen your heart; Wait, I say, on the Lord. Psalm 27:14. NKJV

Unity is powerful. Work together with others to do good.

The Trinity (God, Son, and Holy Spirit) has a singular purpose to save us from our sins. God partners with us to deliver his plan of salvation to the world. Jesus worked with his disciples to fulfill his father's purpose. It's the force of Almighty God against the forces of evil. He has already won.

When you partner with God, you are on the winning team. You are on the team that brings hope to this world and the next. You are no ordinary worker. In God's army, you have extraordinary powers.

What does this mean for your everyday life? Unite with God's people to do good works. Look to him to equip you with the tools to accomplish this. Do not be afraid. He says go. So, go! When you step out each morning, go enthusiastically to partner with others to do God's will.

And above all these put on love, which binds everything together in perfect harmony. Colossians 3:14 ESV

Live in harmony with one another. Do not be haughty, but associate with the lowly. Never be wise in your own sight. Romans 12:16- ESV

Bearing with one another and, if one has a complaint against another, forgiving each other; as the Lord has forgiven you, so you also must forgive. Colossians 3:13 -ESV

You will interact with many people. You must be a team player to join forces with them to do good. Respect them, encourage them, forgive them, and compromise. Do not compromise God's words to create a feeling of solidarity but do everything in your power to humbly contribute to the success of the project or task.

It means that you will not have time to engage in activities contrary to God's love for humanity. You will not have time to be busy with activities without positive eternal value. You will be too focused on producing good works.

Unite with others to further God's plan!

Value the beauty that God has put inside of you. You are special! He made you in his image, and you belong to him.

Look in the mirror. What do you see? Let me tell you. You are a wonder. You are the essence of God's creativity. The love and care of the Father that went into your creation are far beyond man's understanding. Oh, God made you beautiful! God was pleased when he made man in his image. He was delighted with you!

Do not ever take yourself for granted. You are not to be compared to anyone else! You are not to be devalued! You are a prince or a princess, a child of the King!

He knows the strands of hair on your head. Listen! He chose the color of your eyes, your hair, your skin! He did not make a clone and did not want to because He made you unique. He thought about it all, every single detail. Your heavenly Father is proud of his creation, and you should feel proud too.

Every society has its standard of beauty, and this may change from one generation to the next. If you were to travel to different ones, you could get quite confused if you allowed their standards to dictate what you consider attractive. So, don't let the world's varying or ever-changing standards determine what you value. Look to the one who made you. God said that his creation of man was good, so believe him. Value what he loves.

For you formed my inward parts; you knitted me together in my mother's womb. Psalm 139: 13-ESV

I praise you, for I am fearfully and wonderfully made. Wonderful are your works; my soul knows it very well. My frame was not hidden from you, when I was being made in secret, intricately woven in the depths of the earth. Psalm 139:14-15-ESV

Your eyes saw my unformed substance; in your book were written, every one of them, the days that were formed for me, when as yet there was none of them. Psalm 139: 16-ESV

Hardly would a carpenter put effort and creativity into making a table he does not intend to use or sell. He has a purpose for it. This purpose shapes his design. Think of how God made you in a similar light. He intentionally made you for a specific purpose. He made you to glorify him in your unique way, based on your gifts, personality, experiences, challenges, and triumphs. You, dear child, are a masterpiece with a phenomenal destiny like no one has ever experienced. You are unique with the beauty of God inside you!

Your seal reads, *Made in the heart of God.* It does not get any better than that!

Value the authentic brand you are!

Win with God and not by the world's standards. How you play the game or perform is more important than beating others. Do your very best.

God has called you to live a life of integrity. He wants you to work honestly and give your best to please him, not the world. When we only focus on the outcome, we sometimes neglect what God wants us to do because we want the world's approval. We want the world to see us winning, sometimes at the expense of our relationships. You may be tempted to cheat, abandon your responsibilities, or treat people poorly to win or achieve worldly accolades. Resist this because it is not in keeping with what God wants.

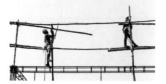

Therefore, my beloved brothers, be steadfast, immovable, always abounding in the work of the Lord, knowing that in the Lord your labor is not in vain. 1 Corinthians 15:58 ESV

I can do all things through him who strengthens me. Philippians 4:13-ESV

Whatever you do, work heartily, as for the Lord and not for men, knowing that from the Lord you will receive the inheritance as your reward. You are serving the Lord Christ. Colossians 3:23-24-ESV

God focuses on your heart. He looks at how you run this race of life. So, do your best according to his principles. Make improvements after each failure or setback, and never give up pursuing God's destiny for your life. When you do this, you will waste less time comparing yourself to others. Comparing yourself to others to try to be better can create feelings of envy or superiority. None of which is in the heart of God for you.

There is no need to strive. God has already won the battle. Christ has conquered the grave and given us the gift of salvation. Run the race of life to please God, not be better or less than your fellow man. He has already defeated the enemy of your soul. Now, walk and work in the victory that the Lord has provided.

Win at life by operating from God's playbook! You do so when you focus on the process, not just the outcome.

Xerox the life of Christ. Living like him is better than doing what your friends do.

Jesus followed his father's teachings and ultimately fulfilled God's destiny for him on earth. What a marvelous gift he provided humankind through his obedience. By obeying God, he saved us from condemnation and eternal death. His commitment to follow God's plan ensured eternal life for us!

Do what the Bible says, not what you think. You are human. You make mistakes. He is perfect. God made you. He knows what is best for you.

But the Holy Spirit produces this kind of fruit in our lives: love, joy, peace, patience, kindness, goodness, faithfulness, Gal 5:22-NLT

But as for me, I will look to the Lord; I will wait for the God of my salvation; my God will hear me. Micah 7:7-ESV

A new commandment I give to you, that you love one another: just as I have loved you, you also are to love one another. John 13:34-ESV

Yes, to God, no to self

You have a purpose.

Give your life to God. You are the created. He is the creator. You were born for a purpose that originated in the heart of God. You were born to bring him glory. You, therefore, have a mission.

As a result of our sinful nature, we tend to be selfish and want to do things our way and for our self-interest. This nature makes us focus solely on what our fleshly desires. Most of this contradicts God's purpose for you. He wants you to love him wholeheartedly, love others, and spend eternity in heaven with him. You cannot save yourself from this. God can and he will if you ask him.

Once you have accepted Christ, you have begun your first and most important steps into the purposeful life for which God created you. Your time is now. You sealed your destiny when you accepted the gift of salvation. You are heaven-bound, so walk with your head held high. You are on the most important mission of your life, and your commander is the Most High God.

Say yes to God's gift of salvation! Relinquish power over yourself and live out your earthly days with God's heavenly power.

For I know the plans I have for you," declares the LORD, "plans to prosper you and not to harm you, plans to give you hope and a future. Jeremiah 29:11-NIV

The Lord will fulfill his purpose for me; your steadfast love, O Lord, endures forever. Do not forsake the work of your hands. Psalm 138:8-ESV

For we are his workmanship, created in Christ Jesus for good works, which God prepared beforehand, that we should walk in them. Ephesians 2:10-ESV

Zoom towards all that God has planned for you.

Live with zeal. Do what God tells you to do!

Run towards God's purpose for you. As a runner fixes his eyes on the finishing line, fix your eyes on the blueprint provided in the bible. Copy what it tells you to do. Follow the perfect example provided by Jesus. Look at the lives lived inside the pages and learn from them. The bible is God's map and personal letter to you. Please read it as carefully as you would a letter from a cherished friend. Read it as tenderly as a soldier on the battlefield reads his letters from home.

Let the scriptures do God's work in your life and mold you into the person he created you to be. Let it show you that God can and will

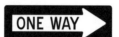

Love is patient and kind; love does not envy or boast; it is not arrogant or rude. It does not insist on its own way; it is not irritable or resentful, it does not rejoice at wrongdoing, but rejoices with the truth. Love bears all things, believes all things, hopes all things, endures all things. 1 Cor. 13:4-7 ESV

But the fruit of the Spirit is love, joy, peace, patience, kindness, goodness, faithfulness, gentleness, self-control; against such things there is no law. Galatians 5:22-23-ESV

And let us not grow weary of doing good, for in due season we will reap, if we do not give up. Galatians 6:9-ESV

Affirm you		
Bless you		
Calm and comfort you		
Discipline and deliver you		
Encourage you		
Free you from negativity		
Guide you		
Help you		
Inspire you		
Justify you		
Keep you grounded		
Launch you into your destiny		
Make you wise		
Nourish your soul		
Organize your priorities		
Produce good works in you		
Quiet all negative thinking		
Refresh your spirit		
Strengthen you		
Teach you		
Unleash your best		
Validate you		
Warm your heart		
X out your sins		
Yank you from despair and destruction		
Zero -in on you because you are SPECIAL to him.		
Zoom to the zenith of God's will and purpose for your life!		

PRAYER OF SALVATION

If, while reading this book or after reading it, you would like to accept Jesus into your life as your personal Savior, read the following prayer or a similar one to start your life on this remarkable journey.

Dear God,

Thank you for creating me. Thank you for loving me. I understand that I was born sinful because of Adam's sin in the Garden of Eden. Because of this, I have done wrong things that have hurt you and others.

I am sorry for my sins. Thank you for sending Jesus to die for my sins. I ask Jesus to come into my heart right now and forgive me of all my sins. I want to serve you and love you, Lord, with all my heart, soul, and mind. Amen

_____   _____
                    Write your name here.   date

Now that you have accepted Christ into your life, heaven is rejoicing that you chose to receive God's best for you. You are now ready to start living life in God's way. What next?

1. Continue to talk to God as you did in the prayer above but now do it using your own words. He does not care how you sound. He wants you to talk to him every day.

2. Get a bible and study what God wants to say to you.

3. Join a Bible-believing church so you can surround yourself with like-minded people who will support you in your journey as a follower of Christ.

4. Share your excitement with others.

Write the bible verses that you will memorize below.

_____

_____

_____

_____

_____

_____

_____

_____

_____

_____

_____

The following discussion questions relate to the content of the book.

1. Which advice do you find easy to follow and why?

_____

_____

2. What kind of help do you think you need in this area to achieve success?

_____

_____

_____

3A. Which advice do you find challenging to follow and why?

_____

_____

_____

_____

3B. How can I help you achieve success in this area?

_____

_____

_____

_____

3C. What are some steps that you can consistently take to achieve success in this area?

_____

_____

_____

_____

Who has done it? God is our ultimate example. There are people in the Bible and in our own lives today who seem to exemplify God's way. Who are they?

Write their name/s below beside the advice given in the book.

A	
B	
C	
D	
E	
F	
G	
H	
I	
J	
K	
L	
M	
N	
O	
P	
Q	
R	
S	
T	

U	
V	
W	
X	
Y	
Z	

My prayer list:

_____ _____

_____ _____

_____ _____

_____ _____

_____ _____

_____ _____

_____ _____

_____ _____

_____ _____

_____ _____

_____ _____

Write the Bible verse that comes to mind for each image below in the space provided.

Find the highlighted words from the scripture in the word search below.

All scripture is breathed out by God and profitable for teaching, for reproof, for correction, and for training in righteousness, that the man of God may be competent, equipped for every good work.

2 Timothy 3:16-17 ESV

```
C U D O O W W B W N I L G V X
X G D O G T R G J J Z E D O T
W V N B T E I F F R F P G N D
I V P I A S Z O Q S V X A M E
M R Y T H E T O O S X R U H T
H T H D K C O R R E C T I O N
Y E G C W S A P A T F M I Q E
D Y F D N C R E V I D T H Q T
E M A P H R T R T E N V Y N E
G O O D I I W H P S Z I A I P
R U B F D P B P P M P K N K M
V V W R A T I Q X S S H D G O
S S E N S U O E T H G I R O C
S G T I Q R H Q W U E Y I F L
U E M E A E L B A T I F O R P
```

Find the words from the scripture verse on the previous page in the crossword below.

ACROSS/HORIZONTAL

3. good for

5. discipline

8. word of God

9. capable

10. practicing to demonstrate a skill

11. just

DOWN/VERTICAL

1. prepared

2. goodness

4. reprimand

6. blew

7. instructing

11. Creator of the universe

Create your own illustration for the title, A-Z Living Life, God's Way. Remove this page and put it in a central area to remind yourself of how to live.

Printed in the United States
by Baker & Taylor Publisher Services